Someday I'll Be a Queen

A Pawn's Journey Across the Chess Board

Christel Minne

Illustrations: Diriq

PART 1

Pompon Pawn Takes Us on an Adventure

In part one a  and small are hidden. Can you find them?

My name is Pompon Pawn,
And I will gladly tell,
Of the strange land I inhabit
And have come to know so well.

I have a full head of spiky hair,
And I'm still just a preschooler,
But this land, one day, if I get my way,
Shall be mine, and I, its ruler.

When you're older, who will you be?
Will you just lay around and watch TV?
I know what I want, I'm leaving this town,
To make it big, and wear a Queen's crown.

Inside my head these dreams of power,
Grow day by day, louder and louder
When it's time to charge forward, my heart will know,
And I'll yell at the top of my lungs and go.

The Chessboard

My land is a board, with squares black and white,
Carried 'round the world by plane and by tide,
Eight squares by eight, a humble terrain,
But battles won on it are seldom in vain.

This isn't a chopping board, like in the kitchen,
Or a whiteboard like the ones in school,
It's a gameboard, tidy and cute,
Learn how to use it if you want to be cool!

The game of chess is a mini-war,
Featuring kings, dragons and more,
A battle which tests your loyalty,
To queens, and knights, and royalty.

When you can play this game,
Everyone will admire your brain,
So let's learn now – but first a story,
Of how a humble pawn can get to glory.

A Very Old Game

This book also tells, if you're curious,
How this game came to pass.
Handed down through centuries,
To be played today by us.

The very first time that chess was played,
Your parents and their parents weren't around,
Nor your house, your dog or your car,
What a strange time! How does it sound?

They had no phones, no street lights,
No iPads, toilet paper or cable TV,
I think you'll agree chess had quite the ride,
To be here today with you and me.

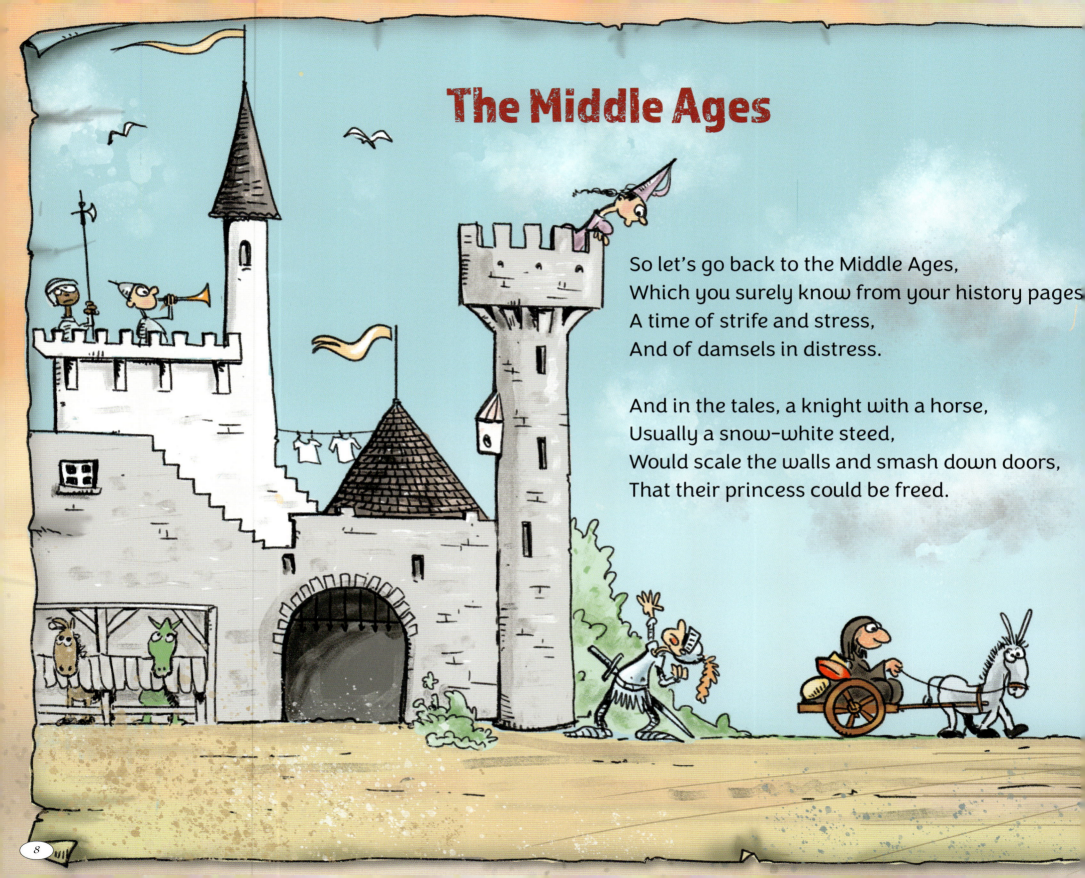

The Middle Ages

So let's go back to the Middle Ages,
Which you surely know from your history pages.
A time of strife and stress,
And of damsels in distress.

And in the tales, a knight with a horse,
Usually a snow-white steed,
Would scale the walls and smash down doors,
That their princess could be freed.

The Encounter

My encounter with the Black King,
Gave me quite the thrill.
He'd been looking for a girl with spiky hair,
And I exactly fit the bill.

He hired me as one of his soldiers,
Since I look before I leap.
So I joined his army, but
I warned him looks don't come cheap.

India

Now let's travel across to India,
Where tigers and elephants roamed,
Far from England or America,
Was where chess found its home.

Amidst the high mountains and deserts,
They used elephants for work and play,
And when an elephant would charge at you,
It was best not to be in the way.

Into this world our game was born,
For battles of a different kind,
That princes, with the push of a pawn
Could show dominance of the mind.

The Black King

The Black King was a sweet man,
Suited for the finer things,
Like chatting, or helping people,
Or simply walking while he sings.

"Isn't life just great?
If you have a problem– I'm all ears,
And I will put a smile on your face,
As your problem disappears."

A merry man, you might conclude,
Although he only wore black.
All his household followed suit,
Trailing black robes at their back.

His clothes were lined with glistening jewels,
Beautiful pearls, flawlessly black.
Even if anyone could notice a stain,
They'd not mention it out of tact.

In his crown lay a giant black diamond,
Darker even than the night.
Its shimmering depths encasing the echo,
Of all that once had been light.

His town was black too,
and so were his roads,
Houses and walls and schools,
All in a grey monochrome.

And yet he was not a sad man,
His kindness and light shone through,
For goodness will always carry the day,
As I know yours will too.

13

The White King

Now the next thing you must know,
Is that next to the Black King's domain,
Lived the perfectionist White King,
Who could not abide a stain.

A little spot here, a wine spill there,
And the poor man would throw a fit,
His clothes always had to be sparkling white,
And he couldn't handle it.

His crown was inlaid with opals,
Always polished for show,
For he had this strange obsession
With looking whiter than snow.

The beads in his clothes, the shoes on his feet,
Would be instantly thrown away,
If once they were dirtied by mud or sand
Kicked up by a child at play.

"My life is so difficult", he sighed.
"I need to control everything.
Can't people pick up their trash, control their dog,
So I can stop with this cleaning?"

The King Is Missing

One day he received a pile of letters,
A gigantic pile of paper,
"I am only going to read the white ones,
Because I find that colour nicer."

"Sir, where were you before?
We looked in all the houses and huts,
The length and breadth of this land,
Even among the children and mutts."

"We yelled and screamed 'til our faces turned blue,
But you're like a snowman hidden in ice,
Invisible by your own design,
A prisoner of your own device."

"And what would you like me to do?"
The King turned and looked at his men.
"Does that mean I should never sit still?
Would all of you be happy then?"

"Instead let's go and ask the Black King
Why his clothes are stained.
I'll organise a trip there for us,
All expenses will be paid."

A Smart Plan

The White King boarded his elephant,
He readied it for attack,
He rode it right out of the palace gates
Saying in the morning he'd be back.

The Black King greeted him as he came,
His mood considerably fresher,
"My old, long-lost friend,
To what do I owe this pleasure?"

"My men are complaining to me,
That I'm too sullen and dour,
I know that I need to up my game,
But I just can't find the power."

"Well, you are a good King,
No worries, no regrets and no shame,
Let's have some fun and you'll be right as rain,
Shall we just make up a game?"

"Let's mix our countries together",
He continued with a smile.
"White and black squares next to each other
Making up each rank and file."

The files going up and down,
and ranks from left to right,
Had four black squares each,
Alternated with four white.

The people stood back to admire,
The work their kings had done.
No need for pointless struggle,
It seemed everyone had won.

Even the White King was happy,
According to his mood,
His men could tour all the white squares
Or stop on the way for food.

A New Name: Pompon Pawn

One fine day the Black King,
Was strolling through the land,
I came out to meet him,
To tell him what I'd planned.

"Pompon, my girl, what's up?
What do you think of this board?
A new idea, so I'm open to critique,
Once you've been round and explored."

"Well, Your Majesty, I can see,
That there are 64 squares all told,
But I'd like to meet my colleagues,
If I may make so bold."

"Great idea", he said with a nod,
"I'll gather you all in a line,
Arrange you in front of me for protection
And move you one at a time."

Then his elephant ambled along beside,
And we started to plan,
Who else we'd need, and when,
Before the game began.

The White King Thinks with Us

"Of course", the White King exclaimed,
When he'd heard of our designs,
He called his finest knight to his side,
And arranged his chariots behind the lines.

"I'll have to move first", he said with a scowl,
"So I guess I'll use two dice,
For I have trouble deciding sometimes,
But can easily throw a six twice."

"If he wants a battle he'll have it,
And surely I will prevail!
But wait! What will be the prize,
And what does winning entail?"

Are You a Good Loser?

"We'll play to capture the King",
Said my boss the Black King with a grin,
"One of us will be trapped on a square,
On every which side hemmed in."

And so we played in good spirits,
And the White King felt victory was assured,
But once his two dice stopped bringing him luck
He threw them outside of the board.

"I'll lose anyway, what is the point?
These things have no place in the game,
You're getting so lucky here,
All I say is it's a shame."

The Black King watched from a distance,
His face its usual grey,
But even he couldn't suppress a laugh,
At this unseemly display.

"Well maybe use your brain then,
Instead of relying on the dice,
And don't be such a sore loser,
It isn't very nice."

To console the White King,
And reduce his sense of shame,
My boss made him an offer,
That White should start every game.

Pompon Pawn Traveling

And so in both the palaces,
Chessboards took pride of place,
And dukes and nobles learned to play,
And win, and lose, with grace.

Visitors to both the courts,
Would see the boards on the rack,
And if they were important enough,
They'd get to take one back.

And I, the humble Pompon Pawn,
Have travelled both steppe and sea,
And while that might seem crazy to you,
It certainly isn't to me.

The Arabs took me on their camels,
And studied the game by night,
But the Vikings from the north,
Gave me more of a fright.

They took me aboard their longships,
And changed the game as they sailed,
And each time they brought it to someone new,
The rules grew more detailed.

Whenever the game reached Europe,
The biggest change came on the board,
Since nobody had ever seen an elephant,
That chess piece was simply ignored.

The Real Game Begins

"Let's pick some new pieces then,
The elephant needs a new name."
The White King discussed with the Black,
And the bishop entered the game.

The Europeans knew chariots, but yet somehow
They had more place in a history book,
So in place of the chariots of India,
Came the tower, or castle, or rook.

I've told you a lot of history,
Maybe more than you need,
So let's start to play, and along the way,
I'll bring you up to speed.

PART 2

How Do Chess Pieces Move.

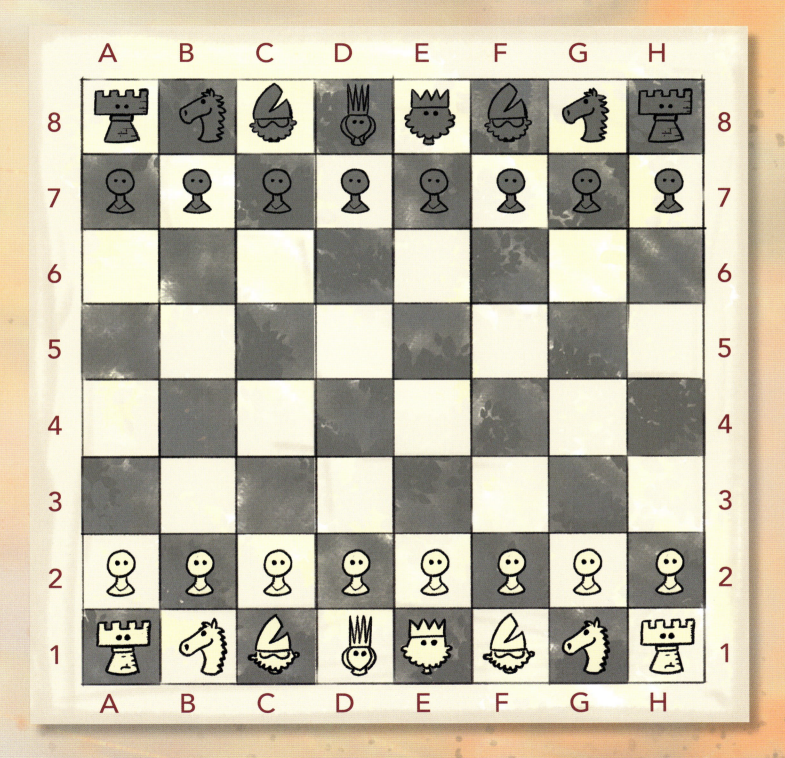

The Steps of the King

In the middle of the rearmost row,
The Black King set up his royal chair.
When pressed as to why he wanted that space,
He replied "Because they'll see me there."

Myself and seven other black pawns,
Were instructed to stand in front of His Grace.
A long sturdy wall of willing soldiers
Linking arms in a strong embrace.

The Kings met up, to discuss the rules,
And both being of advanced age,
It was swiftly agreed to limit their moves,
And leave the other pieces to engage.

A single step, in any direction,
Up, down, right or left.
My King said, "I could manage that,
Without becoming short of breath."

The White King suggested a little change,
Before the armies were told.
A King's move could also be diagonal,
But the new home must border the old.

Kings Don't Take Each Other

"These new rules all seem great,
But I'd like something else besides.
It would be better to have an empty square,
At all times, between you and I."

"Our swords won't hit each other,
For our arms are far too short.
Instead we'll need to plan and use
All the other pieces on the board."

"Let's make a pact to never kill,
For murder is too much.
A King can be encircled
But still immune to touch."

"And we 'take', not eat or kill,
To distance our game from a war,
A piece takes another, and goes to the square,
Where the other one had stood before.

Putting the King in Check and in Checkmate

"A threat against one of the Kings,
Shall have the special name "check",
Everyone else must stop what they're doing
In order to save our neck."

"So one of our army can shield us,
By jumping right into harm's way,
Or we can take the invader,
And remove him from the play."

"To counter such a mortal threat,
The King may also run,
Provided he has somewhere to go,
This is often done."

"And if one of us can't hide from check,
Or block, or take, or flee,
The game ends then, with no bloodshed,
The other side gets victory."

"This special check is called a 'mate',
The players shake hands and smile,
You and I go back to our place,
At opposite ends of a file."

CHECK !

CHECKMATE

Chariots Become Towers

Now I told you before about chariots,
And how the Kings were changing its name.
The Black King didn't want a weapon
To sully his beautiful game.

And while the White King loved his chariot,
He had to eventually agree,
That a castle was perhaps a more peaceful name,
For the reduction of enmity.

Up the walls of a castle
A knight could still climb,
To save a damsel in distress,
And ask her to be his bride.

While today most say "rook",
In place of castle or tower,
The battlements at the top of the piece,
Remind us of its power.

As long as nothing blocks its sight,
The rook moves in straight lines, as we've told,
Up and down and left and right,
An absolute wonder to behold.

Are Those Smart and Fast Elephants Still in the Game?

The White King thought long and hard,
About the other pieces at his command,
The elephants were gracefully retired,
And a replacement was needed in the land.

But before he agreed, the Black King
Did come to seek my counsel,
On whom he should pick for this noble role,
I saw his list, written in pencil.

Bishop, priest, juggler, smith,
Rabbi, general, mercenary.
"Pompon", said the King solemnly,
"Pick one from the list and read it to me."

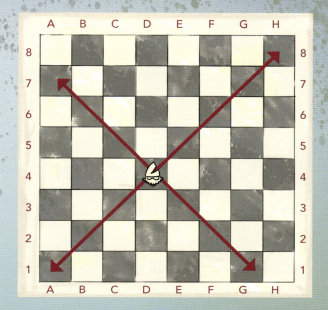

"Thank you Your Majesty, for trusting me",
My finger trembling along the page,
I settled it finally on the first name;
The bishop would join us in this new age.

And as the real bishop is tied to a church,
So the chess piece does limit its might,
From the start of the game, each bishop
Must touch only dark squares, or only light.

The Queen

The Kings quickly discussed,
and reached an accord,
Each side would have two bishops,
One of each sort.

With two bishops, two rooks,
And two knights apiece,
The Kings needed one more
To make the game complete.

"Which other piece should I have?
Your choice", my King asked.
And I understood that this request
Would be my final task.

Before I could answer,
His wife graced the scene,
We looked at each other and knew,
The final piece would be the Queen.

The White King did demur,
For he was stuck in the past,
And didn't quite like the idea
Of his wife moving so fast.

So he went into his royal court,
And had a word with his wife,
She threw a spear at the White King
Who barely escaped with his life.

She told him in no uncertain terms,
That she'd take the left side and he, the right,
No longer would chess be a man's game,
Even if she joined it out of spite.

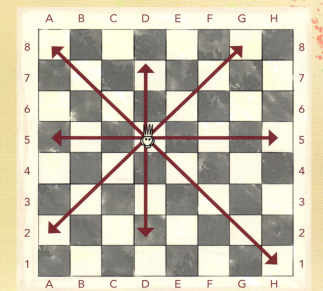

So the White Queen took her place,
and the black one too,
Combining the power of a rook and a bishop
She did what she wanted to do.

Next thing we knew, the board was complete,
The White King flanked by his feisty dame,
The Black King mirroring the same,
And both sides ready to commence the game.

The last little problem: the letter 'K',
Was wanted by the King and one of his men.
Can you guess who? Yes, it's the knight!
"Alright", said the warrior, "I'll take 'N' then."

Qc3 x c5
Rf7-f1

Someday I'll Be a Queen

I'll remind you I'm a soldier girl,
And at heart always have been.
The key question is coming up:
Will I ever be a Queen?

I asked the King, with voice sugar-sweet,
To care closely for us and our dreams.
"Pompon Pawn, you've helped me so much
I'll do my best to make you a Queen."

The White King couldn't conceal his contempt,
He had eight pawns too, blocking all of us,
They each stayed on their own lines,
Each one supporting the others.

I found that a little sad,
That I couldn't move left or right,
And that my way would be blocked,
By the white pawns in their spite.

So I went to the King, to spill my thoughts,
Ever wise, he read my mind,
And told me the rules of being a pawn:
"Look always forward, and never behind."

"When you get to the end, you get to choose,
To be a knight, bishop, rook or Queen,
And when you take, you might get to move,
To a file where you haven't already been."

To tell the truth, I was relieved,
That I captured diagonally as well,
But then I heard yet another rule,
That brought me more joy than I can tell.

The Difficult Horse

And now as the book's nearly over,
It's time to head back to the Knight.
The very hardest piece to master.
Did we plan this book right?

Indeed we did, for quickly you'll learn,
That the Knight moves in the shape of an L,
Two squares one way, then a sharp turn,
Enchanting players with its spell.

A curvy piece in a game of straight lines,
Starting right next to the castle or rook,
Jumping over all the stop signs,
The Knight is the cheekiest piece in the book.

I twist my snout and then watch out:
I jump two steps forward and one aside
That's happens when a Knight is untied.

A Knight in the centre can jump to 8 squares,
In the way that's shown on the right.
We try to keep it there, for better air,
And if it starts on a black square it ends on a white.

Let's Get Started!

So, what did you think?
Is your heart beating faster?
Would you like to learn my game
And maybe become a grandmaster?

A handshake to start and end each match,
For we are no longer at war,
This is merely a board game,
And the result is only a score.

The next step might be my toolbox,
One page at a time, day by day,
Getting to know the pieces,
Which will guide you on your way.

Whenever you play, remember well:
Win or lose, don't scream or yell,
We play in good spirits with a smile on our face,
You make no friends if you call people names.

Old and young, girls and boys,
Buy chess sets for learning, and not just as toys,
Your brain will thank you, as will I,
But for now I bid you goodbye.

Why I Wrote This Book

How Attractive This Game Is!

Many young children find the arrangement and movement of chess pieces on the board to be intriguing, and I very much wanted to provide an extremely gentle guide that would lead them into the world of chess. This desire originated from years of practical experience with 4-5 year olds whom I was teaching the rules of chess, with the aid of (sometimes spontaneous) stories and visual aids. The earnest questions of these future leaders made me want to give a concrete form to the process. As such, I hit upon the idea of making a gripping, rhyming narrative which explains the moves and chessboard geometry, while also being fully illustrated and introducing some (hopefully) new vocabulary. I want children around the world to learn chess (and other things) in playful, easy ways!

Age Range: 4-99+

This picture book and the accompanying toolbox are designed for use by children as young as 4, but older children, parents, grandparents or educators will also enjoy it. You can work through the text and illustrations together, while learning the rudiments of chess without it feeling like 'work'. This reader can be used even by instructors and parents who know nothing about the game, and you will find yourself picking it up naturally along the way!

Some children get 'bitten' by the chess bug, and in some cases you'll find the child ready to devour the whole book in one sitting. This might be due to an older family member who plays (and therefore must be beaten!), a developmental advantage or particular giftedness, an interest in board games, or a condition like ADHD and ASD. In these cases I would urge: Not all at once!! Instead of letting a child work through it in one go, why not build some suspense and mystery; by letting them look forward to the next chapter as a treat, in the long run you keep their interest at a sustainable level.

Working With the Toolbox

Thus, when you're introducing the chess pieces (see chapter 3 in the toolbox) feel free to leave gaps of up to a week before moving onto the next chess piece. During that time, you can play the mini-games relating to all pieces introduced up to that point, and let the group have some good-natured fun with them. It is best to do this only after finishing the picture book, and in my experience the rather non-traditional order I use here (starting with the king, rather than rooks or pawns) makes the most sense.

I've faced questions about that over the years. "That sounds strange", some professional chess coaches have told me, or the more fleshed-out version, "Young children are not yet able to checkmate. They mainly care about capturing pieces." For sure, 4-5 year olds are fixated on capturing pieces and not on the idea of checkmate. But it still feels strange to have a rook, bishop, etc. without mentioning the piece to which the ultimate goal of all others relates: the King.

By starting with the king I create an immediate mental link to the world of castles and princesses, tapping into the interest areas of a typical preschooler (who naturally finds tales of royalty to be fascinating.) Also, the king moves very simply: one step in all directions. This is ideal to start with, as it develops a sense of 'chessboard geometry'. Another important fact is that the king must be protected, and the children find this exciting too. This reinforces the ultimate goal of chess for them.

They only learn how to give check in a later part of the course, but themes of protecting the king from checks as well (run, block, or capture) wind up being discussed during this section too.

More about the toolbox:

Rhyme As a Style Choice

Young children really enjoy rhymes for their own sake, but in this case there is an additional benefit to having the text rhyme. The stanzas (together with the pictorial aids) will help the knowledge stick more firmly in the child's mind, with different children making more use of the text or the illustrations according to their own learning style. In either case, they are more likely to remember the rules and culture of chess during those early friendly games with peers.

Chess History and Practice

This book is divided into two parts. In the first, the history of chess is worked into the story as you are introduced to the characters. While much speculation (and outright fiction) exists around the origins of chess – who invented it? How long has it been around? Etc… – some parts are certain enough that we can add them into the narrative. The chess pieces are brought to life and characters that unlock dimensions in the fantastic mind of a preschooler. More than a few times I've noticed such anthropomorphisms of what a piece has 'said' or 'done' actually guide a child to execute the moves correctly!

In the second, we explain what each chess piece can do and the starting position of the game. According to your child's taste, if you come back to this book for a second time it might make sense to only read the second part. As mentioned before, there is also a toolbox for starting with the more technical part of a child's introduction to this game.

Having Fun is Our Goal!

With the publication of this volume (and the toolbox), I hope to convey the message that playing chess with young children is possible, can be fun and rewarding (for everyone!) and offers holistic benefits to them. I believe it is beneficial to include an introduction to chess on school curricula, and if my guide makes it easier for educators, parents, caregivers or therapists to give children that opportunity, then I will consider that my time has been well spent. Have fun!

About the Author

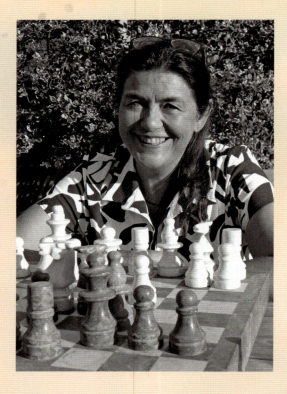

My name is Christel Minne, and for over 3 decades I have been an educator in the municipality of Oostkamp, Belgium. During my career I have been able to experience various roles as a kindergarten teacher, early primary school teacher, counsellor and care assistant (to all age groups.)

The school I work in (Freinetschool Klimop) has incorporated chess into the curriculum, giving all our students the chance to try their hand at learning this special game. I have given many of these chess lessons and discovered a remarkable enthusiasm and eagerness to learn in children from four to twelve years of age. I hold a Class C chess coaching certificate from the Flemish chess association.

There are good children's books about chess, some of which I have used, but usually they breeze straight past the fantasy, intrigue and whimsy (that I believe should be a primary driver of learning) and focus immediately on technical mastery… As such, I decided to turn my own years of chess teaching experience into a guide others could use while filling a definite gap in the market.

Earlier in my career as an educator, I published a didactic method, *Schrijf met heel je lijf* (in Dutch) which teaches children how to write the letters of the alphabet, supporting both visual and kinaesthetic learners in memorising the Latin alphabet and developing good handwriting through a playful and fun approach. Rhyme is also a feature of that book, ensuring that the contents linger longer in the mind of the student. That then translates into better memory of the moves, geometry and intangible skills developed during the learning process. So, in some sense, I had a template of the form (i.e. rhyming verse) and desired results (i.e. playful learning) of *Someday I Will Be a Queen*.

Slowly the conviction grew in my mind that a picture book and toolbox combo was the way forward, giving children (and the adults in their lives) tools for starting to learn chess. Gathering the material while teaching it proved to be a useful aid: my 4-year olds were just finishing up learning about the King, Rook, Bishop and Queen when I went and knocked on the door of my friend Diriq, the illustrator, with whom I have also worked previously, and we started work in earnest.

Before long we were looking for a publisher to help turn the dream into reality, and I found what I was seeking at Thinkers Publishing, a Belgian chess-publisher helmed by Daniël Vanheirzeele, famous in both Europe and the USA for high-quality technical chess books and for their commitment to the vision of each author. This work was first published in Dutch as *Later word ik koningin, 2022*.

We hope this book (and Dutch equivalent) makes it into many households, schools and the like, and enriches the lives of the educators, family members and (of course!) children who read it. I wonder whether it will inspire at least some of today's children to become tomorrow's grandmasters!?